Liberty Phi

AQUARIUS

INTRODUCTION

Astrology is all about the planets in our skies and what energy and characteristics influence us. From ancient times, people have wanted to understand the rhythms of life and looked to the skies and their celestial bodies for inspiration, and the ancient constellations are there in the 12 zodiac signs we recognise from astrology. The Ancient Greeks devised narratives related to myths and legends about their celestial ancestors, to which they referred to make decisions and choices. Roman mythology did the same and over the years these ancient wisdoms became refined into today's modern astrology.

The configuration of the planets in the sky at the time and place of our birth is unique to each and every one of us, and what this means and how it plays out throughout our lives is both fascinating and informative. Just knowing which planet rules your sun sign is the beginning of an exploratory journey that can provide you with a useful tool for life.

Understanding the meaning, energetic nature and power of each planet, where this sits in your birth chart and what this might mean is all important information and linked to your date, place and time of birth, relevant *only* to you. Completely individual, the way in which you can work with the power of the planets comes from understanding their qualities and how this might influence the position in which they sit in your chart.

What knowledge of astrology can give you is the tools for working out how a planetary pattern might influence you, because of its relationship to your particular planetary configuration and circumstances. Each sun sign has a set of characteristics linked to its ruling planet – for example, Aquarius is ruled by Uranus – and, in turn, to each of the 12 Houses (see page 81) that form the structure of every individual's birth chart (see page 78). Once you know the meanings of these and how these relate to different areas of your life, you can begin to work out what might be relevant to you when, for example, you read in a magazine horoscope that there's a Full Moon in Capricorn or that Jupiter is transiting Mars.

Each of the 12 astrological or zodiac sun signs is ruled by a planet (see page 52) and looking at a planet's characteristics will give you an indication of the influences brought to bear on each sign. It's useful to have a general understanding of these influences, because your birth chart includes many of them, in different house or planetary configurations, which gives you information about how uniquely *you* you are. Also included in this book are the minor planets (see page 102), also relevant to the information your chart provides.

AQUARIUS

Our sun sign is determined by the date of our birth wherever we are born, and if you are an Aquarius you were born between January 20th and February 18th. Bear in mind, however, that if you were born on one or other of those actual dates it's worth checking your *time* of birth, if you know it, against the year you were born and where. That's because no one is born 'on the cusp' (see page 78) and because there will be a moment on those days when Aquarius shifts to Pisces, and Pisces shifts to Aries. It's well worth a check, especially if you've never felt quite convinced that the characteristics of your designated sun sign match your own.

The constellation of Aquarius is one of the oldest and largest in our skies. Taking the shape of a water carrier, its story is based on that of the beautiful shepherd Ganymede who was snatched by an eagle and transported to Zeus to become the official water-bearer to the gods. The brightest star in the constellation is Sadalsuud, meaning the luckiest one.

Aquarius is ruled by Uranus, the ancient Greek god of the sky and the first modern planet discovered. Aquarius embodies many of the qualities of this powerful planet of change and innovation, originality and occasionally disruption.

An air sign (like Gemini and Libra), Aquarius is all about ideas and connection. No surprise that many feel we are currently in the age of Aquarius, a period of around 2,000 years, that heralded scientific rationalism and the emergence of internet technologies. Aquarius is also a fixed sign (like Taurus, Leo and Scorpio) and they show a determined, committed edge and an ability to see things through to completion. Because they are also all about the ideas, Aquarius also has an ability to make highly original connections as a route to problem-solving; thinking 'outside the box' comes naturally to many of them. The only downside is that they can sometimes be a little rigid in their thinking, until the next bright idea comes along.

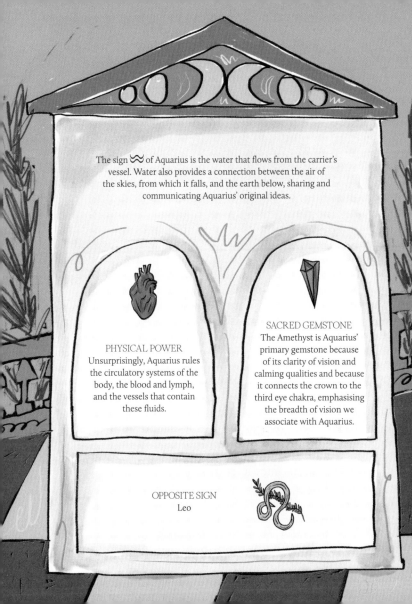

The sign ♒ of Aquarius is the water that flows from the carrier's vessel. Water also provides a connection between the air of the skies, from which it falls, and the earth below, sharing and communicating Aquarius' original ideas.

PHYSICAL POWER
Unsurprisingly, Aquarius rules the circulatory systems of the body, the blood and lymph, and the vessels that contain these fluids.

SACRED GEMSTONE
The Amethyst is Aquarius' primary gemstone because of its clarity of vision and calming qualities and because it connects the crown to the third eye chakra, emphasising the breadth of vision we associate with Aquarius.

OPPOSITE SIGN
Leo

The sign of the water carrier, Aquarius is a gregarious soul, enjoying wide associations and friendships but always independent of heart. They are considered something of a free spirit being the air sign they are, with a commitment to the wider global humanity rather than the individual. Aquarius rules the 11th House of friendship (see page 85) and a truer friend you probably won't find but they won't be pigeonholed in any tribe.

Ruled by Uranus, this powerful planet can sometimes be disruptive and rebellious but that's not always a bad thing, as shaking up the *status quo* helps refresh our thinking. And if an Aquarian suddenly wants to change the rules, they've probably thought it through, so that what seems unexpected can be rooted in some clever ideas. So while it may look like an intuitive spark, that's not how Aquarius operates. The flowing water in this sign's depiction also means there's no risk of stagnation of thought, all of which makes Aquarius a key team player if old strategies are no longer working and new ideas are needed.

This combination of being an air and a fixed sign isn't always a comfortable place to be and can sometimes create inner tension for Aquarius. While originality of ideas lies at the heart of their soul, they can be extremely obstinate, unprepared to change their point of view, so being flexible is often a learnt skill, because it probably won't come naturally. There will inevitably be times when sticking to an idea when it's not working could sabotage the outcome, so it's important for Aquarius to learn to recalibrate and embrace change when necessary.

What makes others tick fascinates Aquarius. They really are a people person but not a people pleaser, as they are too independent for that. Their tendency towards personal independence can also make them appear to be a bit of an outsider. They are always true to their convictions which means that they're seldom swayed by the crowd. However, as a water sign they are able to 'go with the flow' and tolerate the ideas of others even if they disregard them. Their commitment is very much to freedom – freedom of information, speech, human rights and movement – and it's no surprise that the age of Aquarius has seen technology emerge to take these issues global, something Aquarians are keen to embrace.

While friendships are very important, and often with Aquarius there's a real diversity in these because they are open to all sorts of people, being comfortable spending time alone is also an Aquarian trait. Their active mind means there's always plenty to engage with and they are seldom bored, relishing time spent in their own company. When they do socialise they have lots to offer, making them interesting and lively company.

THE MOON IN YOUR CHART

While your zodiac sign is your sun sign, making you a sun sign Aquarius, the Moon also plays a role in your birth chart and if you know the time and place of your birth, along with your birth date, you can get your birth chart done (see page 78). From this you can discover in which zodiac sign your Moon is positioned in your chart.

The Moon reflects the characteristics of who you are at the time of your birth, your innate personality, how you express yourself and how you are seen by others. This is in contrast to our sun sign, which indicates the more dominant characteristics we reveal as we travel through life. The Moon also represents the feminine in our natal chart (the Sun the masculine) and the sign in which our Moon falls can indicate how we express the feminine side of our personality. Looking at the two signs together in our charts immediately creates a balance.

MOON IN AQUARIUS

The Moon spends roughly 2.5 days in each zodiac sign as it moves through all 12 signs during its monthly cycle. This means that the Moon is regularly in Aquarius, and it can be useful to know when this occurs and in particular when we have a New Moon or a Full Moon in Aquarius because these are especially good times for you to focus your energy and intentions.

A New Moon is always the start of a new cycle, an opportunity to set new intentions for the coming month, and when this is in your own sign, Aquarius, you can benefit from this additional energy and support. The Full Moon is an opportunity to reflect on the culmination of your earlier intentions.

NEW MOON
IN AQUARIUS AFFIRMATION

'I am at one with the air and feel its strength lift my heart and soul when I look up and into the sky. I pay heed to its power and trust its ancient currents and energy to support me.'

FULL MOON
IN AQUARIUS AFFIRMATION

'I am born of the air and to the air will I return, and in this knowledge I will relish each breath I take and aspire to do my best.'

AQUARIUS
HEALTH

Aquarius rules the circulatory systems of the blood and lymph. The lower legs, ankles and feet are also a vulnerable area for Aquarius, giving rise to complaints like varicose veins or chilblains, and there can also be problems with breathing which could include problems like asthma. Keeping the leg muscles strong and active also helps balance, another useful area for Aquarius to focus on.

Regular walking is good exercise for Aquarius, allowing them access to fresh air and to stretch their legs, which will help circulation and the lymphatic system, which relies on activity to keep it in good order. Being mentally active is a feature that's often matched by physical activity and many Aquarians are light on their feet with a natural inclination to be active, disinclined to sit still for long. This can be a godsend if work is sedentary as it can provide a reprieve, but Aquarius may also have to look for ways to calm an overactive mind. Yoga, where stretching the limbs and the breath is a feature, can be a good choice, particularly because this is an activity that can be done in a group or alone, while meditation is a skill that promotes a calm mind and mental stability.

POWER UP
YOUR AQUARIUS
ENERGY

There are often moments or periods when we feel uninspired, demotivated and low in energy. At these times it's worth working with your innate sun sign energy to power up again, and paying attention to what Aquarius relishes and needs can help support both physical and mental health.

Because Aquarius is an air sign, their head space can get cluttered with all those original and unpredictable thoughts whizzing about. It's all too easy for air signs to feel disconnected from their physical bodies, which is why a regular practice like yoga, which links the mind to the body through the breath, can be so helpful to many born under the sign of Aquarius. This is also an activity that plays into the greater good of humanity, making it doubly attractive to Aquarius, and can also be done as a group activity or alone. Many under this sun sign definitely enjoy company but often need time out to recharge their batteries. Walking is an activity that can also be done alone or in company, and it affords an opportunity to reconnect to the wider world too, its natural features and the changes in seasons, all of which can be reinvigorating.

Earthing that airy soul will help to keep life stable. It's all too easy for Aquarius to dissipate their energy, casting it to all four winds, so it's important to bear this in mind when looking to power up and utilise those foods and habits that support both body and mind. This means regular meals and hydration – which Aquarius can sometimes forget – which are so important to help balance body and mind, and energise both. Foods that will help with this are those rooted in the earth like carrots, potatoes, beets and parsnips, either juiced or oven roasted and eaten whole. Balance these with light proteins such as fish or poultry, lentils or beans. Caffeinated drinks can aggravate an already active mind, so rebalance this with herbal teas and tisanes to help maintain hydration, along with refreshing H2O, beloved of the water carrier.

When Aquarius needs to power-up, add black pepper to roasted root vegetables, turmeric to lentil soup and cloves to apple crumble, for example – these three spices in particular will help warm and energise the circulatory systems. A yogi tea that combines black peppercorns, cinnamon, cardamom and cloves will also help to refresh and sustain energy, while in the evening lemon balm, chamomile and fresh mint teas will help to calm and relax, which is also necessary.

Utilise a New Moon in Aquarius with a ritual to set your intentions and power up: light a candle, use essential oil of bergamot to stabilise your mood and concentration (this oil blends well with calming chamomile and uplifting vetiver), focus your thoughts on the change you wish to see and allow time to meditate on this. Place your gemstone (see page 13) in the moonlight. Write down your intentions and keep in a safe place. Meditate on the New Moon in Aquarius affirmation (see page 21).

At a Full Moon in Aquarius you will have the benefit of the Sun's reflected light to help illuminate what is working for you and what you can let go, because the Full Moon brings clarity. Focus on this with another ritual, taking the time to meditate on the Full Moon in Aquarius affirmation (see page 21). Light a candle, place your gemstone in the moonlight and make a note of your thoughts and feelings, strengthened by the Moon in your sign.

AQUARIUS' SPIRITUAL HOME

K nowing where to go to replenish your soul and recharge your batteries both physically and spiritually is important and worth serious consideration. For some Aquarians the science lab may be their spiritual home and many may also earn their living in the discovery of new technologies, while others may find their direction in some other way that stimulates their inventiveness and innovation.

Wherever they hail from, there are also a number of countries where Aquarius will feel comfortable, whether they choose to go there to live, work or just take a holiday. These include Finland and Sri Lanka, beautiful Ethiopia and the vast expanse of Russia, all of which reflect the airy energy of Aquarius.

When it comes to holidays, Aquarians often look to wide open spaces where vast skies are evident, from the Pampas of Buenos Aires to the beaches of Brighton or the mountains surrounding Salzburg – all provide the sort of exciting and changeable vistas that help elevate Aquarian mood and allow them to breathe deeply. City breaks also appeal but often where sky meets water like the city of Stockholm.

AQUA

WOMAN

RIUS

This is a woman who is usually highly individual and often easy to spot because her style may verge on the quirky. But even if the colours of her clothes are bright, nothing clashes and her accessories always harmonise. Her look is often very together and may suggest something of an intellectual, because while she wears her intelligence lightly – she is an air sign, after all – the minute she opens her mouth it's apparent this is a smart woman. Not much excites her more than an interesting conversation and she loves to exchange and evolve ideas with those of a similar inclination, making her a fascinating companion.

There's also a certain detachment about Aquarius women. They don't mean to appear aloof at home or at work, but sometimes the world of ideas inside their own heads is so interesting it can take someone quite persistent to help them reveal their warmer side. Her commitment to the wider community in which Aquarius woman lives and works can sometimes look as if it's more important than that of her friends, lovers and family. This isn't entirely true but often Aquarius women can be so involved with saving the planet, they forget how important it is to cherish those closer to home too.

Naturally tolerant and slow to take offence, she doesn't take much personally but as a result can often seem emotionally low-key. Aquarius also rules the 11th House of friendship and there's an easy friendliness and even flirtatiousness that can sometimes belie strength of feeling. She will not give her affections lightly but isn't easy to take for a ride: fool her once and it's unlikely to happen again.

An unpredictable nature is also a feature of Aquarius, and while this can be fascinating and alluring, it can also create something of a challenge to anyone wanting to pursue a friendship or love relationship with her. She may seem an unconventional and light-hearted friend, but she's also a community-minded neighbour and a loyal lover. With Aquarius women it's often an easy friendship that evolves into love, while freedom of expression and thought will always be a key feature of any long-lasting union. So too is love and, once in love, loyalty to their lover and commitment to the relationship is also a feature: once they put their mind to something, it's likely to endure.

A Q U A

N

A

M

R I U S

That interesting conversationalist to whom everyone gravitates at a party? He's quite likely to be Aquarius, radiating goodwill to his companions. This is a man who believes a friend is just a stranger you've not yet met and, gregarious by nature, is the life and soul of a party, because where better to make (more) friends?

This is a man who is likely to be unpredictable too, thanks to Uranus, and rebellious. You can probably see this in the way he dresses. Matching socks? Shirt and tie? Why bother when there's a climate crisis to be solved; his mind is on more important issues. And their approach to problem-solving is likely to be thoughtful, creative and innovative. Not for them the restrictions of society's mores, they want to open things up for the greater good of humankind. But, be warned, this might include a very relaxed attitude to commitment.

Friendship lies at the heart of every relationship an Aquarius man will have: if you can't be friends first, you probably can't be lovers. Understand this and you're half-way to understanding this man's *modus operandi*. So it takes a partner who can recognise this quality without being threatened by it to keep him attached. Freedom of spirit and expression is also key, so expect an honest answer if you hazard a question like, 'Does my bum look big in this?' Aquarius men tend to be very straightforward in their way and don't really do subterfuge, although, because he is so cerebral, he may not always *share* his emotional thoughts. Don't try to second guess him though, a direct question usually elicits a direct answer.

Tolerance is another attribute of this open-minded sign. And while he may tolerate demands made on his time and attention, that doesn't mean he won't walk away if these demands become too much. A serial monogamist, maybe, but as a fixed sign, adaptation to the give and take of relationships doesn't always sit as easily with them as with others, and they will often deliberately avoid excessive emotion. This can make Aquarius men seem rather enigmatic and elusive, making them all the more attractive as a consequence to some, but be warned as what you see is likely to be what you get. Getting them to change is unlikely.

AQUARIUS
IN LOVE

There's a delicious lightness of touch when Aquarius falls in love because they love to love and they thrive on the intellectual energy it generates. It genuinely lifts them, elevating all their endeavours to a higher plane. So if you're on the receiving end of this, it can be a bit of a whirlwind ride but there's also generosity and fun. It may need to be on *their* terms, at least initially, so be prepared for the unexpected. That intimate *dinner à deux* you were planning, and they turn up with three friends? It's partly self-protection in the early stages of falling in love, because they need to be really sure about you before they declare themselves, but also because they genuinely love to share fun times and were *sure* you wouldn't mind! And that's the dilemma that often lies at the heart of loving Aquarius, you have to respect their unpredictable nature and their genuinely wide circle of friends.

AQUARIUS
AS A LOVER

Truly, the best way to secure an Aquarius' love initially is through friendship and shared interests. Non-threatening and with lots of room for conversation, friendship can pave the way towards deeper commitment. It's also helpful if you genuinely share an interest in, for example, something like skydiving (which epitomises the freedom this air sign aspires to). Failing that, allowing them to indulge in activities like these without restriction, and being prepared to hear all about it afterwards, is balm to their soul and will help secure a bond.

What you can expect when they do give their heart is unconditional love, which is quite rare but this is the way they operate. They will love you just the way you are, without endeavouring to mould you to an alternate version. It may take Aquarius some time before they actually realise you're the one, given you were probably 'just a friend' for quite a while, so patience can be a virtue here. But once *they've* decided, they'll let you know in no uncertain terms. However, once they've told you they love you, you may not hear about it again for some time because showy romantic gestures are seldom their forte.

When it comes to sex, Aquarius can be equally as straightforward. Sex is another form of creative expression and all those Aquarian adjectives like experimental, unconventional and rebellious might equally apply. Expect the unpredictable; this is not a lover that looks to a twice-weekly routine and they may surprise you *al fresco* when the mood strikes. Also bear in mind that for them, talk is sexy too. If the word sapiosexual is new to you, look it up, because this is your Aquarian lover to a tee and the mind is as sexual as the body to them.

WHAT'S IN AQUARIUS' BEDSIDE CABINET?

Shibari bondage ties to challenge their love of freedom

Pocket *Kama Sutra*

A multipack of fun lubricants: flavoured, stimulating, soothing

WHICH SIGN SUITS AQUARIUS?

In relationships with Aquarius, the sun sign of the other person and the ruling planet of that sign can bring out the best, or sometimes the worst, in a lover. Knowing what might spark, smoulder or suffocate love is worth closer investigation, but always remember that sun sign astrology is only a starting point for any relationship.

AQUARIUS
AND ARIES

Uranus and Mars are two powerful
planets and the sparks can genuinely
fly in a positive way when they meet,
but there's also a mutual respect for
each other's independence that can
help ensure this bond endures.

AQUARIUS
AND TAURUS

Venus' gentle and grounded approach
to life does much to centre Uranus'
rebellious ways without restricting
Aquarius' freedom, although they are
both fixed signs and can be equally
rather stubborn about what they
believe is right.

AQUARIUS AND
GEMINI

As two air signs, ruled by Uranus and
Mercury, this can be a tempestuous
match with little to ground them.
However, their need to talk things
through is equally balanced and
Gemini is a mutable sign, making
adaptation to Aquarius easier.

AQUARIUS
AND CANCER

The Moon rules Cancer and is able to reflect Uranus' independence without feeling overwhelmed by it, and because Cancer rules the home Aquarius will appreciate returning to its comforts time and time again.

AQUARIUS
AND LEO

Uranus meets its match in Leo's ruling Sun and may find this sign's exuberance and me-first personality too much. And Aquarius' airy indifference to the lion's self-indulgent roar may make this a tricky match, unless both compromise.

AQUARIUS
AND VIRGO

Equally preoccupied by what goes on in their minds, Virgo's Mercury is focused on specifics while Uranus is fixed on a more expansive approach to life. But if they can achieve a balance in these areas, there is much to share and enjoy.

AQUARIUS
AND LIBRA

Uranus has a tendency to upend Libra's commitment to balance and diplomacy, but they are both air signs and recognise the value of talking things through and this relationship benefits from Libra's adaptable nature and Aquarius' tolerance.

AQUARIUS
AND SCORPIO

Both are fixed signs and Pluto can be tricky in association with Uranus, finding Scorpio's need for security at odds with their freedom-loving soul. But Scorpio's transformational energy often attracts Aquarius' unconventional side.

AQUARIUS AND
SAGITTARIUS

Jupiter rules Sagittarius and has all the benefits of an adaptable disposition and love of freedom, which Aquarius finds very attractive. While their air/ fire mix can be combustible there's also an intellectual energy that serves them both well.

AQUARIUS AND CAPRICORN

Heavy-duty Saturn can bring stability to Aquarius, who might experience this as either security or restriction, depending on how these characteristics play out in each. But this air/earth combination can be equally beneficial to both.

AQUARIUS AND AQUARIUS

This is exactly the sort of relationship that might start in a comfortable friendship and grow. The only danger might be in not recognising it for what it is and missing the opportunity for the intimacy it needs for it to thrive.

AQUARIUS AND PISCES

Two dreamers, but Neptune dwells in the imagination rather than the real world of ideas, and Pisces might find Aquarius just too airy and unconventional to latch on to, although Pisces' watery needs may find a safe home with the water carrier.

AQUARIUS
AT WORK

The world of work can sometimes be a tricky place for independent-minded Aquarius. They don't shirk hard work but prefer to work out their own schedules to deliver, factoring in the thinking time they deem necessary. So it can sometimes look as if they are not doing very much, but then they come up with an innovative solution. Strongly creative, this characteristic will leak out – much like water overflowing from its container – into whichever field of work they choose, and thinking 'outside the box' is second nature to many of this sign.

Financial remuneration isn't the driver for Aquarius that it is for some either. They are definitely capable of earning large salaries, but this often comes through the originality of their approach or a new take on an old idea. And they can make surprisingly good investments too, particularly in new technologies. While Aquarius can be an unpredictable employee – because whatever their job description, they are likely to reinvent it – if a boss can hold their nerve, the pay-off can be considerable. What is important for Aquarius is to learn to be a team player, which may not come naturally, but given their commitment to their wider community, Aquarius can learn to work happily with others if it's towards the greater good of the group.

Another facet of this sign is their inclination to look towards occupations that have a humanitarian goal. This can include charity work of course, or careers like teaching, nursing or social work, but can be widened out into scientific goals that benefit mankind. Because of their ability to grasp abstract ideas that can deliver tangible results, the sciences often attract those who are Aquarius or have Aquarius factors strongly present in their chart.

And although diplomacy isn't as strongly featured as for, say, Libra, because Aquarius has such a strong streak of tolerance and decency, they make very equable workmates, and this is important to recognise when it comes to team building. They may be a fixed sign but that often plays out through their ability to stay on a job until it's done, making them surprisingly effective, for all their idiosyncratic approach.

AQUARIUS
AT HOME

Aquarius rules the 11th astrological house of friendship and is a sign usually happy to cohabit with friends or, in some cases, in a commune. Communal living is often a very comfortable place for Aquarius to be. They are not particularly possessive about their space or their material objects and are happy to socialise and eat together with their housemates. What they probably will expect, however, is an equal commitment from all to domesticity. Housework is for everyone, and even the youngest will probably be allocated their regular chores. And recycling – for the good of all – will be a must.

Other than that, Aquarius is likely to have an easy-going approach to their home and likely to prefer a minimalist environment. They do like their gadgets and are attracted by new innovations, so that robotic vacuum cleaner or Wifi heating control will probably be necessities and not luxuries to the Aquarius homemaker. This is also a sign that enjoys spacious surroundings, so the layout might be open-plan with large windows giving rise to airy vistas, and a colour palette of sky or watery blues. But it's also a comfy, welcoming place to be, with carefully selected cushions and carpets often sourced from places to which they've travelled.

That said, cohabitees should be prepared for unexpected guests as Aquarius has a bit of a penchant for spontaneous invites, whether this is for a midweek meal, a weekend visit or a three-month stay. If there's space at the table or a spare room, how better to fill it than with interesting people, old friends and new. Spontaneous and unpredictable is the name of Aquarius' game and their home is open to many, including waifs and strays, such is their innate generosity.

FREE THE
SPIRIT

Understanding your own sun sign astrology is only part of the picture. It provides you with a template to examine and reflect on your own life's journey but also the context for this through your relationships with others, intimate or otherwise, and within the culture and environment in which you live.

Throughout time, the Sun and planets of our universe have kept to their paths and astrologers have used this ancient wisdom to understand the pattern of the universe. In this way, astrology is a tool to utilise these wisdoms, a way of helping make sense of the energies we experience as the planets shift in our skies.

'A physician without a knowledge of astrology has no right to call himself a physician,' said Hippocrates, the Greek physician born in 460 BC, who understood better than anyone how these psychic energies worked. As did Carl Jung, the 20th-century philosopher and psychoanalyst, because he said, 'Astrology represents the summation of all the psychological knowledge of antiquity.'

THE 10 PLANETS

SUN

Although the Sun is officially a star, for the purpose of astrology it's considered a planet. It is also the centre of our universe and gives us both light and energy; our lives are dependent on it and it embodies our creative life force. As a life giver, the Sun is considered a masculine entity, the patriarch and ruler of the skies. Our sun sign is where we start our astrological journey whichever sign it falls in, and as long as we know which day of which month we were born, we have this primary knowledge.

MOON

RULES THE ASTROLOGICAL SIGN OF CANCER

We now know that the Moon is actually a natural satellite of the Earth (the third planet from the sun) rather than a planet but is considered such for the purposes of astrology. It's dependent on the Sun for its reflected light, and it is only through their celestial relationship that we can see it. In this way, the Moon in each of our birth charts depicts the feminine energy to balance the masculine sun's life force, the ying to its yang. It is not an impotent or subservient presence, particularly when you consider how it gives the world's oceans their tides, the relentless energy of the ebb and flow powering up the seas. The Moon's energy also helps illuminate our unconscious desires, helping to bring these to the service of our self-knowledge.

MERCURY

Mercury, messenger of the gods, has always been associated with speed and agility, whether in body or mind. Because of this, Mercury is considered to be the planet of quick wit and anything requiring verbal dexterity and the application of intelligence. Those with Mercury prominent in their chart love exchanging and debating ideas and telling stories (often with a tendency to embellish the truth of a situation), making them prominent in professions where these qualities are valuable.

Astronomically, Mercury is the closest planet to the sun and moves around a lot in our skies. What's also relevant is that several times a year Mercury appears to be retrograde (see page 99) which has the effect of slowing down or disrupting its influence.

VENUS

The goddess of beauty, love and pleasure. Venus is the second planet from the sun and benefits from this proximity, having received its positive vibes. Depending on which astrological sign Venus falls in your chart will influence how you relate to art and culture and the opposite sex. The characteristics of this sign will tell you all you need to know about what you aspire to, where you seek and how you experience pleasure, along with the types of lover you attract. Again, partly depending on where it's placed, Venus can sometimes increase self-indulgence which can be a less positive aspect of a hedonistic life.

MARS

This big, powerful planet is fourth from the sun and exerts an energetic force, powering up the characteristics of the astrological sign in which it falls in your chart. This will tell you how you assert yourself, whether your anger flares or smoulders, what might stir your passion and how you express your sexual desires. Mars will show you what works best for you to turn ideas into action, the sort of energy you might need to see something through and how your independent spirit can be most effectively engaged.

JUPITER

Big, bountiful Jupiter is the largest planet in our solar system and fifth from the sun. It heralds optimism, generosity and general benevolence. Whichever sign Jupiter falls in in your chart is where you will find the characteristics for your particular experience of luck, happiness and good fortune. Jupiter will show you which areas to focus on to gain the most and best from your life. Wherever Jupiter appears in your chart it will bring a positive influence and when it's prominent in our skies we all benefit.

SATURN

Saturn is considered akin to Old Father Time, with all the patience, realism and wisdom that archetype evokes. Sometimes called the taskmaster of the skies, its influence is all about how we handle responsibility and it requires that we graft and apply ourselves in order to learn life's lessons. The sixth planet from the sun, Saturn's 'return' (see page 100) to its place in an individual's birth chart occurs approximately every 28 years. How self-disciplined you are about overcoming opposition or adversity will be influenced by the characteristics of the sign in which this powerful planet falls in your chart.

URANUS

RULES THE ASTROLOGICAL SIGN OF AQUARIUS

The seventh planet from the sun, Uranus is the planet of unpredictability, change and surprise, and whether you love or loathe the impact of Uranus will depend in part on which astrological sign it influences in your chart. How you respond to its influence is entirely up to the characteristics of the sign it occupies in your chart. Whether you see the change it heralds as a gift or a curse is up to you, but because it takes seven years to travel through a sign, its presence in a sign can influence a generation.

NEPTUNE

Neptune ruled the sea, and this planet is all about deep waters of mystery, imagination and secrets. It's also representative of our spiritual side so the characteristics of whichever astrological sign it occupies in your chart will influence how this plays out in your life. Neptune is the eighth planet from the sun and its influence can be subtle and mysterious. The astrological sign in which it falls in your chart will indicate how you realise your vision, dream and goals. The only precaution is if it falls in an equally watery sign, creating a potential difficulty in distinguishing between fantasy and reality.

PLUTO

Pluto is the furthest planet from the sun and exerts a regenerative energy that transforms but often requires destruction to erase what's come before in order to begin again. Its energy often lies dormant and then erupts, so the astrological sign in which it falls will have a bearing on how this might play out in your chart. Transformation can be very positive but also very painful. When Pluto's influence is strong, change occurs and how you react or respond to this will be very individual. Don't fear it, but reflect on how to use its energy to your benefit.

YOUR SUN SIGN

Your sun or zodiac sign is the one in which you were born, determined by the date of your birth. Your sun sign is ruled by a specific planet. For example, Aquarius is ruled by Uranus but Gemini by Mercury, so we already have the first piece of information and the first piece of our individual jigsaw puzzle.

The next piece of the jigsaw is understanding that the energy of a particular planet in your birth chart (see page 78) plays out via the characteristics of the astrological sign in which it's positioned, and this is hugely valuable in understanding some of the patterns of your life. You may have your Sun in Aquarius, and a good insight into the characteristics of this sign, but what if you have Neptune in Leo? Or Venus in Aries? Uranus in Virgo? Understanding the impact of these influences can help you reflect on the way you react or respond and the choices you can make, helping to ensure more positive outcomes.

If, for example, with Uranus in Taurus you are resistant to change, remind yourself that change is inevitable and can be positive, allowing you to work with it rather than against its influence. If you have Neptune in Virgo, it will bring a more spiritual element to this practical earth sign, while Mercury in Aquarius will enhance the predictive element of your analysis and judgement. The scope and range and useful aspect of having this knowledge is just the beginning of how you can utilise astrology to live your best life.

PLANETS IN TRANSIT

In addition, the planets do not stay still. They are said to transit (move) through the course of an astrological year. Those closest to us, like Mercury, transit quite regularly (every 88 days), while those further away, like Pluto, take much longer, in this case 248 years to come full circle. So the effects of each planet can vary depending on their position and this is why we hear astrologers talk about someone's Saturn return (see page 100), Mercury retrograde (see page 99) or about Capricorn (or other sun sign) 'weather'. This is indicative of an influence that can be anticipated and worked with and is both universal and personal. The shifting positions of the planets bring an influence to bear on each of us, linked to the position of our own planetary influences and how these have a bearing on each other. If you understand the nature of these planetary influences you can begin to work with, rather than against, them and this information can be very much to your benefit. First, though, you need to take a look at the component parts of astrology, the pieces of your personal jigsaw, then you'll have the information you need to make sense of how your sun sign might be affected during the changing patterns of the planets.

YOUR BIRTH CHART

With the date, time and place of birth, you can easily find out where your (or anyone else's) planets are positioned from an online astrological chart programme (see page 110). This will give you an exact sun sign position, which you probably already know, but it can also be useful if you think you were born 'on the cusp' because it will give you an *exact* indication of what sign you were born in. In addition, this natal chart will tell you your Ascendant sign, which sign your Moon is in, along with the other planets specific to your personal and completely individual chart and the Houses (see page 81) in which the astrological signs are positioned.

A birth chart is divided into 12 sections, representing each of the 12 Houses (see pages 82–85) with your Ascendant or Rising sign always positioned in the 1st House, and the other 11 Houses running counter-clockwise from one to 12.

ASCENDANT OR RISING SIGN

Your Ascendant is a first, important part of the complexity of an individual birth chart. While your sun sign gives you an indication of the personality you will inhabit through the course of your life, it is your Ascendant or Rising sign – which is the sign rising at the break of dawn on the Eastern horizon at the time and on the date of your birth – that often gives a truer indication of how you will project your personality and consequently how the world sees you. So even though you were born a sun sign Aquarius, whatever sign your Ascendant is in, for example Cancer, will be read through the characteristics of this astrological sign.

Your Ascendant is always in your 1st House, which is the House of the Self (see page 82) and the other houses always follow the same consecutive astrological order. So if, for example, your Ascendant is Leo, then your second house is in Virgo, your third house in Libra, and so on. Each house has its own characteristics but how these will play out in your individual chart will be influenced by the sign positioned in it.

Opposite your Ascendant is your Descendant sign, positioned in the 7th House (see page 84) and this shows what you look for in a partnership, your complementary 'other half' as it were. There's always something intriguing about what the Descendant can help us to understand, and it's worth knowing yours and being on the lookout for it when considering a long-term marital or business partnership.

THE
12
HOUSES

While each of the 12 Houses represent different aspects of our lives, they are also ruled by one of the 12 astrological signs, giving each house its specific characteristics. When we discover, for example, that we have Capricorn in the 12th House, this might suggest a pragmatic or practical approach to spirituality. Or, if you had Gemini in your 6th House, this might suggest a rather airy approach to organisation.

1ST HOUSE

RULED BY ARIES

The first impression you give walking into a room, how you like to be seen, your sense of self and the energy with which you approach life.

2ND HOUSE

RULED BY TAURUS

What you value, including what you own that provides your material security; your self-value and work ethic, how you earn your income.

3RD HOUSE

RULED BY GEMINI

How you communicate through words, deeds and gestures; also how you learn and function in a group, including within your own family.

4 TH HOUSE

RULED BY CANCER

This is about your home, your security
and how you take care of yourself and
your family; and also about those family
traditions you hold dear.

5 TH HOUSE

RULED BY LEO

Creativity in all its forms, including fun
and eroticism, intimate relationships and
procreation, self-expression
and positive fulfilment.

6 TH HOUSE

RULED BY VIRGO

How you organise your daily routine, your
health, your business affairs, and how you
are of service to others, from those
in your family to the workplace.

7 TH HOUSE

RULED BY LIBRA

This is about partnerships and shared
goals, whether marital or in business,
and what we look for in these to
complement ourselves.

8 TH HOUSE

RULED BY SCORPIO

Regeneration, through death and rebirth,
and also our legacy and how this might be
realised through sex, procreation
and progeny.

9 TH HOUSE

RULED BY SAGITTARIUS

Our world view, cultures outside our
own and the bigger picture beyond our
immediate horizon, to which we travel
either in body or mind.

10TH HOUSE

RULED BY CAPRICORN

Our aims and ambitions in life, what we aspire to and what we're prepared to do to achieve it; this is how we approach our working lives.

11TH HOUSE

RULED BY AQUARIUS

The house of humanity and our friendships, our relationships with the wider world, our tribe or group to which we feel an affiliation.

12TH HOUSE

RULED BY PISCES

Our spiritual side resides here. Whether this is religious or not, it embodies our inner life, beliefs and the deeper connections we forge.

THE FOUR
ELEMENTS

The 12 astrological signs are divided into four groups, representing the four elements: fire, water, earth and air. This gives each of the three signs in each group additional characteristics.

FIRE

ARIES ~ LEO ~ SAGITTARIUS

Embodying warmth, spontaneity and enthusiasm.

WATER

CANCER ❧ SCORPIO ❧ PISCES

Embody a more feeling, spiritual and intuitive side.

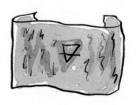

EARTH

TAURUS ❧ VIRGO ❧ CAPRICORN

Grounded and sure-footed and sometimes rather stubborn.

AIR

GEMINI ~ LIBRA ~ AQUARIUS

Flourishing in the world of vision, ideas and perception.

FIXED,
CARDINAL OR
MUTABLE?

The 12 signs are further divided into three groups of four, giving additional characteristics of being fixed, cardinal or mutable. These represent the way in which they respond to situations.

FIXED

TAURUS, LEO, SCORPIO AND AQUARIUS ARE FIXED SIGNS

Their energy tends to be steady and they are less reactive, more responsive, although they can have a tendency to be resistant to change and need encouragement.

CARDINAL

ARIES, CANCER, LIBRA AND CAPRICORN ARE CARDINAL SIGNS

Their energy is often instinctive and action-oriented, enabling them to get things started, although there's sometimes a tendency to fail to carry things through.

MUTABLE

GEMINI, VIRGO, SAGITTARIUS AND PISCES ARE MUTABLE SIGNS

The clue here is their adaptability and responsiveness to change, which they don't fear, and readiness to listen to and embrace new ideas.

MERCURY RETROGRADE

This occurs several times over the astrological year and lasts for around four weeks, with a shadow week either side (a quick Google search will tell you the forthcoming dates). It's important what sign Mercury is in while it's retrograde, because its impact will be affected by the characteristics of that sign. For example, if Mercury is retrograde in Gemini, the sign of communication that is ruled by Mercury, the effect will be keenly felt in all areas of communication. However, if Mercury is retrograde in Aquarius, which rules the house of friendships and relationships, this may keenly affect our communication with large groups, or if in Sagittarius, which rules the house of travel, it could affect travel itineraries and encourage us to check our documents carefully.

Mercury retrograde can also be seen as an opportunity to pause, review or reconsider ideas and plans, to regroup, recalibrate and recuperate, and generally to take stock of where we are and how we might proceed. In our fast-paced 24/7 lives, Mercury retrograde can often be a useful opportunity to slow down and allow ourselves space to restore some necessary equilibrium.

SATURN RETURN

When the planet Saturn returns to the place in your chart that it occupied at the time of your birth, it has an impact. This occurs roughly every 28 years, so we can see immediately that it correlates with ages that we consider representative of different life stages and when we might anticipate change or adjustment to a different era. At 28 we can be considered at full adult maturity, probably established in our careers and relationships, maybe with children; at 56 we have reached middle age and are possibly at another of life's crossroads; and at 84, we might be considered at the full height of our wisdom, our lives almost complete. If you know the time and place of your birth date, an online Saturn return calculator can give you the exact timing.

It will also be useful to identify in which astrological sign Saturn falls in your chart, which will help you reflect on its influence, as both influences can be very illuminating about how you will experience and manage the impact of its return. Often the time leading up to a personal Saturn return is a demanding one, but the lessons learnt help inform the decisions made about how to progress your own goals. Don't fear this period, but work with its influence: knowledge is power and Saturn has a powerful energy you can harness should you choose.

THE MINOR
PLANETS

S un sign astrology seldom makes mention of these 'minor' planets that also orbit the sun, but increasingly their subtle influence is being referenced. If you have had your birth chart done (if you know your birth time and place you can do this online) you will have access to this additional information.

Like the 10 main planets on the previous pages, these 18 minor entities will also be positioned in an astrological sign, bringing their energy to bear on these characteristics. You may, for example, have Fortuna in Leo, or Diana in Sagittarius. Look to these for their subtle influences on your birth chart and life via the sign they inhabit, all of which will serve to animate and resonate further the information you can reference on your own personal journey.

AESCULAPIA

Jupiter's grandson and a powerful
healer, Aesculapia was taught by
Chiron and influences us in what
could be life-saving action, realised
through the characteristics of the sign
in which it falls in our chart.

BACCHUS

Jupiter's son, Bacchus is similarly
benevolent but can sometimes lack
restraint in the pursuit of pleasure.
How this plays out in your chart
is dependent on the sign in which
it falls.

APOLLO

Jupiter's son, gifted in art, music and
healing, Apollo rides the Sun across
the skies. His energy literally lights up
the way in which you inspire others,
characterised by the sign in which it
falls in your chart.

CERES

Goddess of agriculture and mother of
Proserpina, Ceres is associated with
the seasons and how we manage cycles
of change in our lives. This energy is
influenced by the sign in which it falls
in our chart.

CHIRON

Teacher of the gods, Chiron knew all about healing herbs and medical practices and he lends his energy to how we tackle the impossible or the unthinkable, that which seems difficult to do.

DIANA

Jupiter's independent daughter was allowed to run free without the shackles of marriage. Where this falls in your birth chart will indicate what you are not prepared to sacrifice in order to conform.

CUPID

Son of Venus. The sign into which Cupid falls will influence how you inspire love and desire in others, not always appropriately and sometimes illogically but it can still be an enduring passion.

FORTUNA

Jupiter's daughter, who is always shown blindfolded, influences your fated role in other people's lives, how you show up for them without really understanding why, and at the right time.

HYGEIA

Daughter of Aesculapia and also associated with health, Hygeia is about how you anticipate risk and the avoidance of unwanted outcomes. The way you do this is characterised by the sign in which Hygeia falls.

MINERVA

Another of Jupiter's daughters, depicted by an owl, will show you via the energy given to a particular astrological sign in your chart how you show up at your most intelligent and smart. How you operate intellectually.

JUNO

Juno was the wife of Jupiter and her position in your chart will indicate where you will make a commitment in order to feel safe and secure. It's where you might seek protection in order to flourish.

OPS

The wife of Saturn, Ops saved the life of her son Jupiter by giving her husband a stone to eat instead of him. Her energy in our chart enables us to find positive solutions to life's demands and dilemmas.

PANACEA

Gifted with healing powers, Panacea provides us with a remedy for all ills and difficulties, and how this plays out in your life will depend on the characteristics of the astrological sign in which her energy falls.

PSYCHE

Psyche, Venus' daughter-in-law, shows us that part of ourselves that is easy to love and endures through adversity, and your soul that survives death and flies free, like the butterfly that depicts her.

PROSERPINA

Daughter of Ceres, abducted by Pluto, Proserpina has to spend her life divided between earth and the underworld and she represents how we bridge the gulf between different and difficult aspects of our lives.

SALACIA

Neptune's wife, Salacia stands on the seashore bridging land and sea, happily bridging the two realities. In your chart, she shows how you can harmoniously bring two sides of yourself together.

VESTA

Daughter of Saturn, Vesta's job was to protect Rome and in turn she was protected by vestal virgins. Her energy influences how we manage our relationships with competitive females and male authority figures.

VULCAN

Vulcan was a blacksmith who knew how to control fire and fashion metal into shape, and through the sign in which it falls in your chart will show you how you control your passion and make it work for you.

FURTHER READING

Jung's Studies in Astrology: Prophecies, Magic and the Qualities of Time,

Liz Greene, Routledge (2018)

Lunar Oracle: Harness the Power of the Moon,

Liberty Phi, OH Editions (2021)

Metaphysics of Astrology: Why Astrology Works,

Ivan Antic, Independently published (2020)

Parkers' Astrology: The Definitive Guide to Using Astrology

in Every Aspect of Your Life,

Julia and Derek Parker, Dorling Kindersley (2020)

USEFUL WEBSITES

Alicebellastrology.com
Astro.com
Astrology.com
Cafeastrology.com
Costarastrology.com
Jessicaadams.com

USEFUL APPS

Astro Future
Co-Star
Moon
Sanctuary
Time Nomad
Time Passages

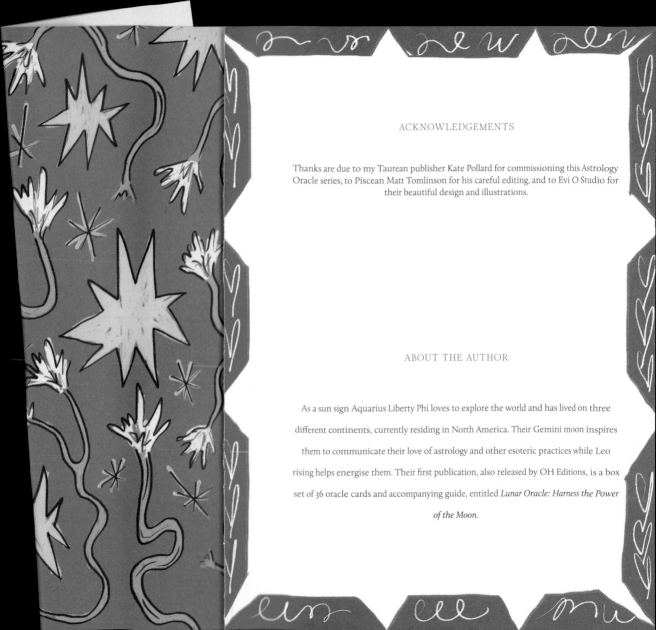

ACKNOWLEDGEMENTS

Thanks are due to my Taurean publisher Kate Pollard for commissioning this Astrology Oracle series, to Piscean Matt Tomlinson for his careful editing, and to Evi O Studio for their beautiful design and illustrations.

ABOUT THE AUTHOR

As a sun sign Aquarius Liberty Phi loves to explore the world and has lived on three different continents, currently residing in North America. Their Gemini moon inspires them to communicate their love of astrology and other esoteric practices while Leo rising helps energise them. Their first publication, also released by OH Editions, is a box set of 36 oracle cards and accompanying guide, entitled *Lunar Oracle: Harness the Power of the Moon*.

Published in 2023 by OH Editions,
an imprint of Welbeck Non-Fiction Ltd,
part of the Welbeck Publishing Group.
Offices in London, 20 Mortimer Street, London, W1T 3JW,
and Sydney, 205 Commonwealth Street, Surry Hills, 2010.
www.welbeckpublishing.com

Design © 2023 OH Editions
Text © 2023 Liberty Phi
Illustrations © 2023 Evi O. Studio

A CIP catalogue record for this book is available from the British Library.

ISBN 978-1-80453-003-0

Publisher: Kate Pollard
Editor: Sophie Elletson
In-house editor: Matt Tomlinson
Designer: Evi O. Studio
Illustrator: Evi O. Studio
Production controller: Jess Brisley
Printed and bound by Leo Paper

ACKNOWLEDGEMENTS

Thanks are due to my Taurean publisher Kate Pollard for commissioning this Astrology Oracle series, to Piscean Matt Tomlinson for his careful editing, and to Evi O Studio for their beautiful design and illustrations.

ABOUT THE AUTHOR

As a sun sign Aquarius Liberty Phi loves to explore the world and has lived on three different continents, currently residing in North America. Their Gemini moon inspires them to communicate their love of astrology and other esoteric practices while Leo rising helps energise them. Their first publication, also released by OH Editions, is a box set of 36 oracle cards and accompanying guide, entitled *Lunar Oracle: Harness the Power of the Moon*.

Published in 2023 by OH Editions,
an imprint of Welbeck Non-Fiction Ltd,
part of the Welbeck Publishing Group.
Offices in London, 20 Mortimer Street, London, W1T 3JW,
and Sydney, 205 Commonwealth Street, Surry Hills, 2010.
www.welbeckpublishing.com

Design © 2023 OH Editions
Text © 2023 Liberty Phi
Illustrations © 2023 Evi O. Studio

A CIP catalogue record for this book is available from the British Library.

ISBN 978-1-80453-003-0

Publisher: Kate Pollard
Editor: Sophie Elletson
In-house editor: Matt Tomlinson
Designer: Evi O. Studio
Illustrator: Evi O. Studio
Production controller: Jess Brisley
Printed and bound by Leo Paper

MIX
Paper | Supporting
responsible forestry
FSC® C020056
www.fsc.org

10 9 8 7 6 5 4 3 2 1

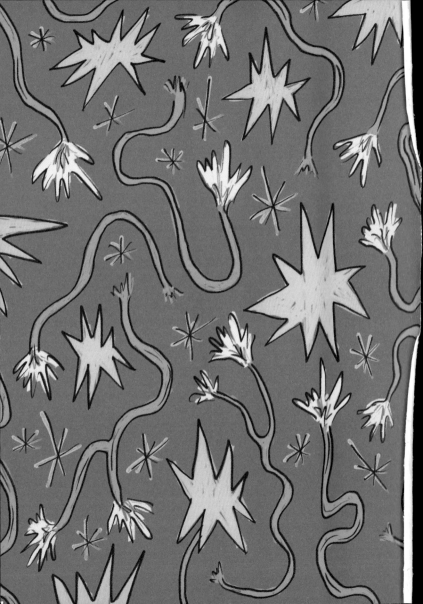